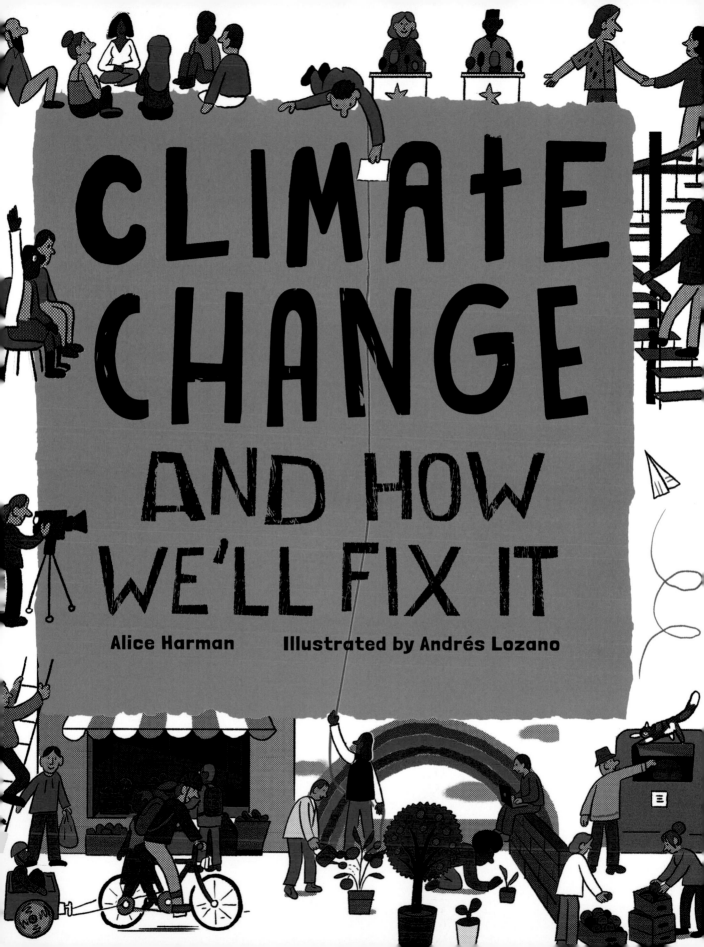

CLIMATE CHANGE
AND HOW
WE'LL FIX IT

Alice Harman   Illustrated by Andrés Lozano

STERLING CHILDREN'S BOOKS
New York

An Imprint of Sterling Publishing Co., Inc.
122 Fifth Avenue
New York, NY 10011

ISBN 978-1-4549-4277-1

Distributed in Canada by Sterling Publishing
Canadian Manda Group, 664 Annette Street, Toronto, Ontario, Canada, M6S 2C8

For information about custom editions, special sales, and premium and corporate purchases, please contact Sterling Special Sales at 800-805-5489 or specialsales@sterlingpublishing.com.

Manufactured in China

Lot #:
10 9 8 7 6 5 4 3 2 1
12/20

www.sterlingpublishing.com

MIX
Paper from
responsible sources
FSC® C008047

CONTENTS

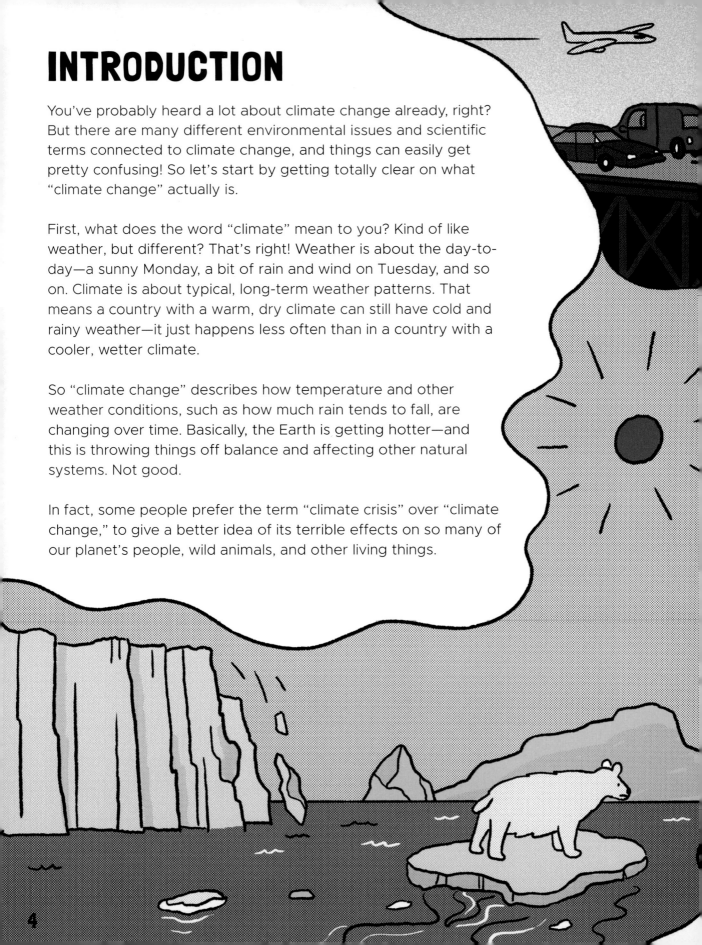

INTRODUCTION

You've probably heard a lot about climate change already, right? But there are many different environmental issues and scientific terms connected to climate change, and things can easily get pretty confusing! So let's start by getting totally clear on what "climate change" actually is.

First, what does the word "climate" mean to you? Kind of like weather, but different? That's right! Weather is about the day-to-day—a sunny Monday, a bit of rain and wind on Tuesday, and so on. Climate is about typical, long-term weather patterns. That means a country with a warm, dry climate can still have cold and rainy weather—it just happens less often than in a country with a cooler, wetter climate.

So "climate change" describes how temperature and other weather conditions, such as how much rain tends to fall, are changing over time. Basically, the Earth is getting hotter—and this is throwing things off balance and affecting other natural systems. Not good.

In fact, some people prefer the term "climate crisis" over "climate change," to give a better idea of its terrible effects on so many of our planet's people, wild animals, and other living things.

In the first section of this book, we're going to try to answer the big questions you might have about climate change. Questions like "How do we know it's happening?", "What is causing it?", and "What will happen if we don't stop it?"

Then, in the second section, we'll look at some of the problems getting in the way of fixing climate change. And in the third section, we'll try to figure out how humans—including you!—can help solve these problems and create a better, safer world for us all.

You might notice that, throughout this book, some words (especially the sciencey ones) are in **bold**. This means that you can check what they mean in the glossary on pages 62–63.

One last, very important thing before you read on—try to remember that although climate change is worrying, it's also fixable. Scientists have told us so. We just need to work together to make the changes we need to, as soon as we possibly can. Got it? Good. See you on the next page!

The greenhouse effect

You might have heard people talking about "the greenhouse effect" and "greenhouse gases," but what exactly does all this mean—and how is it connected to climate change?

What is the greenhouse effect?

It's lovely and warm inside this greenhouse, just right for these tomato plants. They wouldn't survive outside—it's too cold.

A greenhouse's clear glass or plastic walls let in the Sun's light, which warms the air inside. But heat can't pass back out through the walls—it's trapped inside!

Now imagine the Earth is in a giant greenhouse. But instead of solid glass walls, this greenhouse has different layers of gases stretching all around our planet—we call this Earth's atmosphere.

"Greenhouse gases" in the atmosphere let in the Sun's light but stop too much of its heat from escaping back out into space. When everything's in balance, this is a good thing. It keeps Earth at a warm, steady temperature.

Without the greenhouse effect, there'd be no life on Earth!

The problem is that human activities are now producing too much of these greenhouse gases, such as **carbon dioxide**, methane, and nitrous oxide. This traps too much heat in our atmosphere, warming up the planet to unsafe temperatures.

> **Although they have a big impact, all the greenhouse gases together only make up around 1% of Earth's atmosphere. Most of the atmosphere is made up of nitrogen (78%) and oxygen (21%).**

What does this mean for Earth?

It's tricky to **predict** exactly how these changes to Earth's atmosphere will affect our planet, but scientists think we can expect general temperature rises across the world. And because our planet has lots of complicated natural systems that intertwine and affect each other in different ways, this global warming is likely to have worrying impacts such as:

* rising sea levels, partly caused by vast ice sheets melting, that will put islands and coastal cities at risk of flooding
* **droughts** and fires in areas that are already hot and dry
* more rain in some areas, causing floods
* the death of plants and animals that can't adapt quickly enough to the changing climate
* more powerful storms and other extreme weather events

Over the next few pages, we'll look at some of the main ways that humans are generating greenhouse gases—and what needs to change in order to stop, or at least slow down, climate change.

Energy and fuel

We need energy to light up our homes and cities, to cook our food and keep ourselves warm, and to power all sorts of machines from smartphones to trains to huge pieces of factory equipment. All this energy has to come from somewhere!

Energy sources

We can generate energy from "clean," **renewable** sources—such as the Sun, the wind, the ocean waves, and Earth's underground heat—without pumping out lots of greenhouse gases and other pollution.

Or we can get energy from burning "dirty" **fossil fuels**— such as **crude oil**, natural gas, and coal—formed over millions of years deep below the Earth's surface. This second option releases huge amounts of greenhouse gases into the atmosphere, as well as other forms of dangerous air pollution that harm people's health.

Seems like a pretty obvious choice to drop the fossil fuels, right? Lots of people agree, and there are large-scale campaigns to leave fossil fuels in the ground and focus on only using renewable energy sources.

In order to prevent Earth's temperature rising more than 3.6°F (2°C), scientists have said that we need to leave around two-thirds of our fossil fuel reserves in the ground and never burn them.

> We need to keep developing wind farms, solar farms, and other energy systems so they can replace more and more fossil fuels as soon as possible. But we also need to think about how best to use the precious energy we have.

A waste of energy

One major issue is that the world's richer countries use—and waste—a huge amount of energy. From people leaving lights and electronics turned on when they don't need them, to companies selling goods that don't use energy **efficiently**, rich countries' current energy use is far higher than it needs to be.

Another big issue is that most transport vehicles, from airplanes and cars to trucks and ships, still use fuels made from crude oil. So whenever a company transports goods around the world for shoppers to buy, or a person takes a flight to go on vacation, or the owner of a gasoline-powered car drives instead of walking, cycling, or taking **public transportation**, this pumps out greenhouse gases.

People and businesses need to be careful not to waste energy thoughtlessly, but we also need to make sure that products and buildings are designed to use energy as efficiently and cleanly as possible. For example, some newer cars now run partly or entirely on electricity, and houses can be **insulated** so they need less heating to stay warm.

Food and farming

Everyone needs to eat, but our planet just can't handle how we produce and consume food at the moment. While global food businesses make huge amounts of money, and shoppers in richer countries enjoy a wide variety of products from all over the world, the environment is suffering and struggling.

Attack of the killer cow farts!

It sounds silly, but cow burps and farts are a really serious problem when it comes to climate change. Herds of cattle raised for meat and dairy products release lots of methane, a powerful greenhouse gas.

To make matters worse, cows also need space for grazing and for growing crops to feed them—and cutting or burning down forests is a cheap way to create this space. Trees **absorb** carbon dioxide and give out oxygen, so getting rid of these forests doesn't just mean killing precious animals and plants—it also destroys one of our greatest natural defenses against climate change.

Producing meat and dairy uses a lot more land and energy than growing plants to eat. If everyone on Earth stopped consuming **animal products**, we could use 75% less farmland and still feed the world.

Although people in richer countries can help the environment by choosing to eat animal products—especially beef—much less often, there are lots of other issues to be aware of, too.

Food waste

Around a third of all food ends up being wasted. That means all the energy used to farm, **process**, transport, package, and display that food is wasted, too—so a lot of greenhouse gases were pumped into the atmosphere for no reason. Companies need to avoid wasting food before it is ever sold, but shoppers can also help cut food waste by planning meals and using up leftovers.

Industrial farming

Earth's soils may contain up to three times as much carbon as our atmosphere, and we need to keep the soil healthy to avoid this carbon being released into the air. Industrial farming methods—such as growing a single crop over huge areas and using lots of chemical fertilizers and pesticides—are designed to produce more food in the short term, but they could end up destroying soil health and reducing how much food we can grow in the long term.

Unhealthy, overworked, chemically poisoned soil can end up stripped of the water, nutrients, and complex **ecosystems** that crops need to grow. This could lead to a vicious cycle of relying on ever more destructive farming methods to produce enough food crops.

Too much stuff

What do we really need to live, apart from the air we breathe? Clean water, food, and shelter, sure. Some clothes, too. But while hundreds of millions of people still don't have enough, others are buying far too many things they don't need—and our planet can't keep up.

The shopping cycle

Big companies make lots of money by convincing people that they need to buy more stuff, newer stuff, better-looking stuff—even if what they have still works perfectly well. Many items—from clothes to electronic devices—are often not designed to last for very long, and can be difficult, expensive, or even impossible to repair or **recycle** properly.

All this unnecessary "stuff" is often quickly thrown away, restarting the whole shopping cycle. And many products go unsold and are discarded before they're ever used. Not only is this a huge waste of all the energy and environmental damage that goes into the making, **packaging**, and transport of these products, it also generates massive amounts of garbage.

The average person uses almost three times more natural resources—such as trees, metals, and fossil fuels—than they did around 50 years ago. People in the richest countries use up to 10 times more resources than people in the poorest countries.

Of course, some materials can be recycled—and a few countries now recycle over half of their waste. But most of the world's waste is still either burned, releasing carbon dioxide and other harmful gases into the atmosphere, or left in **landfill** sites. Many countries are running out of space to put landfills, and sites also give off greenhouse gases—such as methane—as natural materials break down.

PLASTIC PROBLEM

Another issue isn't just how much stuff we're producing and wasting, but what that stuff is made from. Plastics can cause environmental damage at every stage of their life cycle, and yet companies keep on producing and selling huge amounts of plastic goods and packaging.

Fossil fuels are extracted, transported, and processed to make plastics.

Plastic material is made into goods and packaging for sale. These items are transported, generating more greenhouse gases.

Waste plastic is burned, giving off carbon dioxide.

Waste plastic goes to landfills, where it may take hundreds of years to break down.

Only 20% of the world's plastic waste is recycled.

Waste plastic ends up in the ocean, making the water more **acidic**.

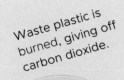

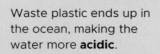

Evidence of climate change

So how do we actually know that climate change is happening? The short answer is: because scientists around the world have collected data and carried out research that shows us it is.

By studying measurements taken from weather stations, ships and buoys out on the ocean, and research stations in Antarctica, scientists have found that Earth's average surface temperature has risen by around 1.8°F (1°C) over the last 140 years or so—mostly in the last 40 years. This might not sound like much, but it's big, bad news.

Satellite science

Scientists can also clearly see other changes in our warming climate. For example, **satellites** circling and photographing Earth show areas of ice and snow shrinking over time. These changes are getting more drastic, too—in 2018, scientists found that ice in Antarctica was melting three times faster than it had been before 2012.

The 2010s were the hottest decade on Earth since records began in 1880.

Satellites bounce radio waves off the sea, too, to measure how much the sea level is rising. Over the last 100 years, the global sea level has risen about 8 inches (20 cm)—and it's rising at a greater speed every year.

Still not convinced?

Some people accept that Earth's temperature has generally risen over the last century but still don't believe that climate change is really a problem—or that humans are behind it. They point out that Earth's temperature naturally rises and falls over time, and that extreme weather events such as floods and droughts are nothing new.

This is true. So why do 97% of working climate scientists agree that human activities are extremely likely (more than 95%) to be the cause of our planet's recent, drastic warming?

Well, scientists can see what temperatures, climate patterns, and greenhouse gas levels were like at different times in the past by studying natural records. These can be rocks, corals, fossils, the rings of tree trunks, and the gas bubbles and solid particles trapped in ice cores—long chunks of ice—drilled from deep within Earth's ice sheets. And they appear to show that when greenhouse gas levels rise, so does Earth's temperature; when they fall, the temperature falls.

This matches what we know about the greenhouse effect (see pages 6–7). And as human activities over the last century have generated ever more greenhouse gases, we've seen temperatures climbing much higher than scientists believe they would on their own.

Impact of climate change

If we don't take action on climate change now, scientists predict that things will only get worse. Although experts are wary of saying that any one heatwave, flood, hurricane, or forest fire is directl caused by climate change, studies have found tha they all seem to be happening more often.

Climate injustice

The really unfair part? It's the world's poorest people, who generate the fewest greenhouse gas **emissions**, who are likely to suffer climate change's most serious effects. For example, millions of people rely on growing small amounts of food to feed themselves, and if their crops die because of too-hot, too-dry conditions, then they might have to leave their homes—if they are able.

Poorer countries are also less likely to have the money to protect their people against the effects of climate change, with measures such as flood defenses, or to rebuild and recover after extreme weather events.

Many people have already had to flee their homes because of rising sea levels, natural disasters, and other environmental changes. Experts predict that over 140 million people could be "climate **migrants**" by 2050.

Feedback loops

Scientists worry that climate change may also throw Earth's systems so off-balance that it triggers natural "feedback loops"—vicious cycles that cause runaway climate change.

1. Disappearing ice

Large areas of white ice on Earth's surface reflect sunlight back into space, helping to cool our planet. But they're melting into darker ocean water, which absorbs more heat. This heats up the Earth, meaning more ice melts.

2. Ocean acidification

Oceans naturally absorb carbon dioxide, but higher levels—plus plastic pollution in the water—have made the water far more acidic. Not only does this threaten sea life, it may also stop the ocean from giving off sulfur gas that helps cool the atmosphere. Warmer oceans then in turn absorb less carbon dioxide.

3. Forest fires

Hotter, drier conditions can make forest fires more common and widespread. These fires give off lots of carbon dioxide and also destroy trees that would otherwise absorb carbon dioxide. This heats up the Earth, raising the risk of forest fires even further.

Why aren't we fixing it?

As you've learned in the last few pages, climate change is a really big problem. But luckily, scientists have told us what actions we need to take—so problem solved, right? Well no, not quite. Unfortunately things aren't that straightforward...

The truth is, we've actually known how to solve climate change for a while now, and yet the climate crisis keeps getting worse.

If we know what to do, why aren't we just doing it? That would seem like the sensible course of action. But the reality is that people, and the ways in which our world works, can be very complicated.

There are all sorts of different points of view, reactions, interests, and arguments that are stopping or slowing down efforts to fix the climate crisis. Some of them might seem frustratingly illogical, selfish, or short-sighted—and, honestly, sometimes they might be!

But we're facing such a huge, global challenge that we need as many people, governments, companies, and organizations as possible to work together to fix it. This means that we have to try to understand what is behind the reluctance to act on what scientists tell us we need to do.

By exploring both sides of some of the biggest issues and arguments around solving the climate crisis, we can better understand not just what we need to do but how we can realistically get it done in a positive way that includes the interests of as many people as possible.

Over the next few pages, we'll look at some of the biggest problems that are currently holding up progress through a series of conversations. You'll see that although adults often talk about politics, economics, and social issues as "grown-up stuff," some of the human behaviors at work might be a lot more familiar to kids than adults might like to think...

The "Just one more cookie" problem

Have you ever been tempted to take "just one more" cookie even though you weren't really hungry? It might explain why some businesses make decisions that harm the environment.

Let's listen to a climate **activist** talking to the global head of a huge fashion chain store...

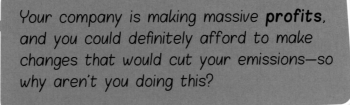

Your company is making massive **profits**, and you could definitely afford to make changes that would cut your emissions—so why aren't you doing this?

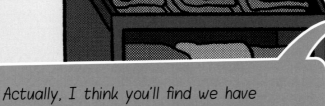

Actually, I think you'll find we have recently taken positive steps to become more green—for example, we now sell a range of organic cotton T-shirts.

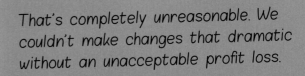

Seriously? How about some changes that will actually make a difference? Like only selling clothes made of recycled material? Or just selling fewer clothes?

That's completely unreasonable. We couldn't make changes that dramatic without an unacceptable profit loss.

But that's the point! You make millions in profits every year—surely it's worth sacrificing some of that money to do your part in stopping climate change?

We're a business, not a charity. We need to make bigger profits every year to keep our **investors** happy. That's how our success as a company is measured.

Then that definition of success needs to change! You can't keep growing and growing, making more and more money, at the expense of the planet and everyone living on it.

Well, it's not up to our company to change it. Even countries measure their success by their economic growth—if they're getting richer, that's a good thing. And as our company grows, we provide more jobs too.

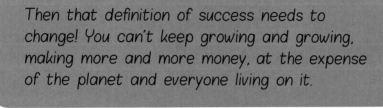

The PROBLEM:

When it comes to business, we tend to think that bigger means better. Our financial system rewards businesses when they grow, and companies that need outside investors are under pressure to maximize their profits—if they don't, they risk losing their investors and going out of business. So if it's a choice between protecting the environment or making more money, Earth will usually lose out. Some companies accept making smaller profits in order to be more eco-friendly, but they often operate on a much smaller scale. Governments can pass laws forcing companies to clean up their act, but they worry about risking jobs and economic growth, too.

Find some solutions on pages 46-47, 48-49, 56-57, and 58-59.

The "That's not fair!" problem

Have you ever been told, "Life isn't fair?" Well, it's true: some people, and some countries, have more than others. Let's listen to the leader of a rich country talking to the leader of a much poorer country...

Hey! Why are you building power stations that burn coal? Haven't you heard of global warming?

Ha! Everybody knows that your country has been burning coal for hundreds of years.

But now we're stopping. We're moving to new green power sources, like solar. You need to do the same thing.

Your country is rich partly because you used your natural resources— including coal. We have the right to make our country richer too.

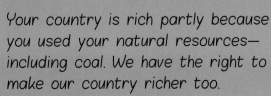

That will have to wait—making people richer means using more energy, and the planet can't cope with that.

But that's not fair! One person in your country uses more energy than 100 people in my country. And for us, getting richer doesn't mean fancier houses or bigger wardrobes of clothes—we're talking basic food, medicine, and so on.

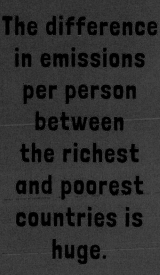

The difference in emissions per person between the richest and poorest countries is huge.

This is no time to be pointing fingers. Climate change is a problem for all of us.

One year's CO₂

But you created this problem! You're the ones who should fix it, not us. And we can't afford new green technologies—if you want that to happen, you need to give us money to help.

One year's CO₂

Find some solutions on pages 44-45, 52-53, and 54-55.

The PROBLEM:

While rich countries try to cut emissions, many poorer countries are working to improve living standards—which usually goes hand-in-hand with increased **consumption** and "dirty" polluting technologies. But people in poorer countries point out that they have the right to enjoy the same quality of life as rich parts of the world—which got rich in the first place partly through polluting activities.

The "Would I lie to you?" problem

How can some big companies justify continuing to do the very things that scientists tell us are responsible for climate change? Let's listen in on a TV interview with a spokesperson for the fossil fuel industry.

Listen, Earth's climate has always changed—it's natural. If global warming is really a problem, how come we still get cold weather?

Isn't that a misleading argument? Weather and climate aren't the same thing. And scientific experts have linked Earth's rising temperature to all sorts of extreme weather, from roasting heatwaves to harsher winters.

Ha! A few years ago these "experts" were panicking us about the "hole in the **ozone layer**," but that's magically stopped being a problem. Now they're scaring everyone about "climate change" instead.

There was nothing magical—the hole in the ozone layer got better because of a massive international effort to stop producing harmful **CFC** gases. And scientists have clear **evidence** to back up their climate concerns.

Well, we have scientists who tell us that climate change is not an issue at all and that the fossil fuel industry is already doing enough to keep the planet safe.

What do you say to people who argue that most of your scientists who reject climate change aren't actually experts in climate science?

Irrelevant. The real issue is the "renewable energy" sector spreading lies to turn people against fossil fuels because they can't beat us fairly—wind and solar power are too expensive to be a realistic option.

Hmm, recent reports actually suggest that wind and solar power are now the cheapest possible power sources. But we'll have to leave it there.

The PROBLEM:

Polluting industries have billions to fund a slick, far-reaching network that spreads misinformation and undermines trust in climate experts. Many people—including politicians and other powerful figures—may prefer to believe in this climate change denial, and it's easy to see why. Climate change is scary, and it'd be lovely to enjoy life without worrying about it. Wouldn't it be reassuring to believe that everything was fine, and that anyone going on and on about humanity needing to make serious changes was just a big liar?

Find some solutions on pages 48-49.

The "Smelt it, dealt it" problem

Poo-eey! All right, who's responsible for letting rip all these gas emissions? Well, it depends how you measure a country's emissions: should you just look at what it makes, or all the things it buys?

Let's sit in on a conversation between the leaders of countries on either side of this argument...

Countries like mine have worked hard to cut our emissions over recent years, but you're canceling out our progress by generating more and more pollution.

Um, do you mean the pollution caused by making things that people in rich countries buy?

If developing countries are going to make money producing those goods, they're responsible for managing the environmental impact that comes with it.

Actually, I think you'll find that countries such as India and China, which produce so many goods, still manage to have lower per-person greenhouse gas emissions than the richer countries where they're sold.

But we're trying to head in the right direction, with measurable targets for cutting our emissions, and we need everyone to do the same.

Those targets are based on passing your emissions on to us, though. You don't have to factor in nearly so much pollution from sourcing raw materials and creating goods in factories because we do that work for you.

Well, what do you want us to do about it? You wouldn't want us to stop our **consumers** and businesses buying things from your country, would you?

You could start by setting honest emissions targets that include the pollution from products you **import** into your countries.

Find some solutions on pages 52-53 and 54-55.

The PROBLEM:

Global climate change plans often set national targets for cutting emissions and punish countries that fail to meet their targets. But when a poorer country makes things for sale in a richer one, who is responsible for the emissions? Is it fair to pay someone else to do your dirty work, and then claim it has nothing to do with you? Poorer countries argue that it's unfair for richer countries to get credit for cutting their emissions when they haven't really changed their eco-unfriendly behavior—just pushed it overseas.

The "You always take their side" problem

In a **democracy**, every voting person in the country is supposed to get an equal say in how the country is run. But in reality a powerful, wealthy person can have a huge amount of influence over what governments do.

Let's listen to this chat between a newly elected politician and the head of a climate action group.

> Your election campaign received large donations from people in the coal industry, and you meet regularly with coal industry **lobbyists**. Doesn't this close relationship get in the way of your responsibility to protect people from climate change?

> Not at all! Politicians have to meet with industry experts to be able to understand the issues. And their campaign donations make elections fairer—otherwise, only rich people would be able to afford to run for office.

> But now you're blocking new green **taxes** that would make the coal industry pay for emissions... Surely the coal industry should pay to clean up its own mess, rather than taxpayers footing the bill for government action to cut emissions?

Businesses and investors create wealth, which benefits all of us. The government needs to step back, giving important industries freedom to grow and innovate.

But your government gives **subsidies** to the coal industry—that's active support, not stepping back! Why should the public pay billions each year to polluting companies?

Subsidies keep energy prices affordable for ordinary people. We pay millions each year to support renewable sources of energy, too.

But renewable energy gets far less help than fossil fuels, even though scientists say we should invest in green energy to reduce emissions. You're just helping out your friends in the coal industry!

The PROBLEM:

Wealthy individuals and businesses often donate huge amounts of money to political campaigns and pay for a vast lobbying network to try to influence government policy. If climate action is not in these people's interest, then the planet and the majority of its people could suffer from the decisions politicians make. Some people may argue that that's just the way the world works, but others believe we can change this unfair system.

Find some solutions on pages 48-49 and 56-57.

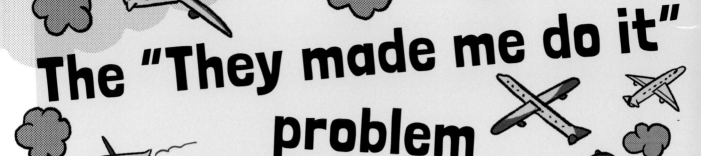

The "They made me do it" problem

Companies often justify their polluting activities by saying they're simply responding to their customers' needs and demands. Many politicians also avoid making tough decisions on climate change that they believe will anger voters.

Let's sit in on this argument between two friends—a local politician and a development manager for a major airline...

> Look, flying is one of the fastest-growing sources of emissions—and yet plane tickets cost around half what they did 40 years ago!

> It's not our fault that people want to fly. Cheaper tickets let more people see the world and visit family and friends abroad. Is it fair to make that a luxury only rich people can enjoy?

> No, but we have to take serious action— like limiting people to a set number of flights per year, or raising flight taxes and using the money to make eco-friendly transport like trains more affordable.

Trains can take way longer than flights, and it's not fair to make hard-working people spend ages traveling when they want to enjoy their vacations.

But most people never get on a plane. Even in rich countries, around half the population takes no flights at all. And yet everyone suffers the environmental impact—especially the world's poorest.

Well why not make meat or new clothes so expensive that only a few people can afford them, then? That would cut emissions too, but I don't see you arguing for that...

I have to balance climate action with doing what voters want. If I go too far, they'll vote me out, and then I won't be able to do anything to help them or the environment.

The PROBLEM:

Find some solutions on pages 46-47, 50-51, 52-53, and 58-59.

Many companies and politicians protest that they can't take action to fight climate change without unfairly restricting people's rights to choice and affordability. But continuing **unsustainable** practices, such as increasing numbers of flights, prioritizes the rights of a small group of people over all humans' rights to live safely on Earth. Politicians need to lead efforts to stop climate change, even if that means making tough, unpopular decisions. However, they need voters to recognize the importance of their representatives acting for this greater good.

The "Goody-two-shoes' problem

Do you like being bossed around and made to feel bad? Probably not. Many people get defensive or dismissive about efforts to fix climate change because they feel like they're being unfairly attacked or talked down to by those involved.

Let's eavesdrop on this argument between a grown-up brother and sister at a family party...

> Rob, what's all this? Balloons, plastic cutlery... I asked you to keep things eco-friendly.

> Ugh, don't start! It's a party, you're ruining everyone's fun with all your 'eco-warrior' whining.

> Oh, I'm sooo sorry for caring about Earth! I guess you want your kids to inherit a dying, trash-filled planet?

> What, so either people do exactly what you say or they don't care about anything? I've got a busy job and three young kids—I don't have the time or money to make things by hand or search online for eco-friendly stuff.

Climate action is everyone's responsibility. We all have to make sacrifices and extra effort wherever we can.

What about your vacation in India? You act all perfect and nag everyone to give up stuff that's fun or convenient for them, but you won't do the same.

I'm not saying I'm perfect, but at least I'm trying! I paid to plant trees to offset my flight's emissions. And I'm not going to apologize for encouraging others to make better choices, too.

You're judging, not encouraging! And **'carbon offsetting'** doesn't really cancel out your flight's damage—you're just paying to stop feeling guilty. We can't all make the choices you do—you complain about me driving to work, but it would take an extra hour and three buses to get there otherwise.

The PROBLEM:

Find some solutions on pages 44-45, 46-47, and 50-51.

People who are passionate about the environment can get frustrated and end up alienating the very people they want to convince to join them. Making eco-friendly choices can often take more effort, and sometimes more time and money, and if people feel nagged and judged for not being "perfect" they may be turned off from trying at all—or from adding their voices to calls for meaningful, large-scale change.

The "Magical homework machine" problem

Technology today is pretty amazing. It can connect people all over the world, bring us an almost-endless stream of information, and save lives through incredible medical advances.

But can it solve the climate crisis for us? Let's sit in on a chat between a "tech believer" and her friend, who isn't quite so sure.

> *Look how far renewable energy has come in recent years. Technology progresses so quickly now—it'll solve the climate crisis soon.*

> *We can't rely on technology to fix everything! We need to change the systems and behaviors causing this crisis.*

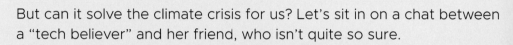

> *Be realistic—most people and companies aren't going to change their ways. We should focus our money and energy on developing new climate technologies, not forcing through impossible changes.*

> *It's not realistic to trust in untested technologies! For instance, we don't really know whether any hi-tech ideas for removing carbon from the atmosphere can practically work on a large enough scale to make a real difference.*

We'll never make progress by dismissing new solutions before we try them. Governments need to invest in developing the most promising climate technologies.

I know it's comforting to believe "clever inventors" will solve everything, but aren't we just looking for excuses to keep using fossil fuels? And why should governments pay to fix a problem while polluting industries keep profiting from making it worse?

Because technology could change the situation overnight—it's in everyone's interest!

But untested, extreme technologies like **geoengineering** might not work—and could make things worse. We already know how to safely stop climate change, we just need to tackle the social and political obstacles.

Some people trust that a miraculous hi-tech climate solution will soon come along, saving the planet without requiring us to make any big changes. This can make the hard work that needs to be done now seem pointless. But relying on shiny new "savior" technologies is a huge gamble: they might not work, and could have unpredictable, serious effects on Earth's complex systems. Even if they were successful, letting our destructive habits continue might mean we face similar or worse problems in the future. By doing the hard work to cut emissions now, we can minimize this risk while still developing new technologies.

The PROBLEM:

Find some solutions on pages 48-49, 56-57, and 58-59.

The "La la la, I can't hear you" problem

Climate change is often talked about by politicians and in the media as a future problem to prevent. But Earth's temperature has already risen and many people are suffering from the effects.

Let's listen in on a discussion at a climate conference between representatives from a rich country and a poor country.

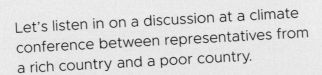

Our shared future is at risk from climate change. We need to agree on targets for reducing emissions and realistic steps we can take to prevent future harm.

This "future" is already here for many poorer countries—particularly those with tropical climates and populations that rely on farming. Our food crops are failing and our people are suffering.

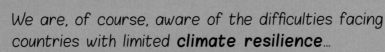

*We are, of course, aware of the difficulties facing countries with limited **climate resilience**...*

And yet you still talk about climate change as a future problem. Does it only count when it starts to affect people in rich countries?

Of course not, climate change affects us all. We've come together at this conference to make action plans to stop it.

But a timeline that works for your country is deadly for mine. If your people were going hungry and being forced from their homes, it would be considered an emergency.

We can't solve climate change overnight, but we're working together to achieve our goals.

These goals are based on richer countries' needs, though! You ignore our calls for urgent funding, yet ask us to leave our forests intact to act as **carbon sinks** for your emissions. It's not fair, we need these resources to make money and provide citizens with food and jobs.

The PROBLEM:

Countries around the world are not experiencing climate change equally. The world's richest, most polluting countries are often least vulnerable to the effects of climate change, and they can seem more focused on avoiding future problems for their people than on helping countries facing present, urgent danger. Many people are frustrated by the cautious pace of global plans when the climate crisis is already causing widespread suffering.

Find some solutions on pages 44-45, 52-53, and 54-55.

The "I won't until you do" problem

Negiotiating global climate plans can be a long, tricky process. But there is an alternative: unilateral action, in which individual countries commit to certain goals no matter what anyone else does.

Politicians aren't always keen on this idea, though—let's listen to this chat between a politician and a local citizen concerned about climate change, to hear why that might be...

This government takes climate change very seriously, but unilateral action isn't a realistic solution. Yes, we'd cut our emissions, but any reduction we make will be canceled out by other countries.

But we'd be setting an example that other countries could then follow. They'd be able to see that our plans had been realistic and effective.

There's no guarantee of that; it's too big a risk. As the government, we're responsible for protecting our country's **economy**.

But what's the point in being the richest country in a dying world? Surely climate change takes priority over the economy?

Look, making major cuts to our emissions would mean bringing in new rules—such as carbon taxes and fines—to stop businesses from polluting so much. What's to stop those businesses just moving to another country and taking their jobs and money with them?

But if every country thinks that way, nothing will ever change—somebody has to take the first step.

Climate change is a global problem, we can't solve it alone. And emissions could actually rise if businesses head to countries with fewer environmental rules—this is called *"carbon leakage."* So it's not just a simple "economy versus environment" choice, you see.

The PROBLEM:

Find some solutions on pages 44-45, 46-47, and 50-51.

Countries are often reluctant to take unilateral climate action, such as introducing stricter limits and higher taxes on polluting companies. They worry that other countries will not make similar commitments and will "steal away" businesses that would rather pollute freely and not pay for it. Although supporters of unilateral action argue that it speeds up progress and can set a good example, others say it is pointless as any progress is canceled out by rising emissions in other countries.

The "Why should I?" problem

Fighting climate change can sometimes seem to ask a lot of us—and it can be frustrating to still see some people doing whatever they want without any thought for the environment.

Let's listen in on this couple talking about whether it's worth bothering "doing your bit" for climate action...

Why should we buy an electric car instead of a big, comfy **SUV**? We can't solve climate change alone, and most people don't seem to care, so all these "eco-efforts" are doomed to fail anyway.

If everyone thought that way, we'd never make any progress! We can inspire other people to make better choices through our own actions.

Nah, I reckon the really rich and powerful people are taking us all for fools. We're so caught up feeling guilty and pointing fingers at each other that we don't notice they're still zipping around the world in private jets and making fortunes off polluting the world.

I get what you're saying, but compared to the majority of people in the world, we are rich and powerful.

Whatever we do is still just a drop in the ocean. The future is looking really scary, so why not enjoy ourselves and have a bit of luxury now?

Because we have a duty to live as greenly as we can, and to push for change on a higher level.

It's the same problem again, though—if only a few of us are pushing for change, politicians and businesses on this "higher level" are never going to listen. It's a waste of time unless there are loads of us.

The PROBLEM:

Many people can feel like there's no point taking climate action because others don't seem to care, so any impact will be too small to make a real difference. And if there's nothing they can do about climate change destroying everything, why not relax and enjoy some eco-unfriendly comforts before things start getting really bad? Giving up hope can end up looking pretty similar to just not caring.

Find some solutions on pages 44-45, 50-51, 56-57, and 58-59.

What we have to do

Adults love to tell kids how they should behave and treat one another, but they're not always great at remembering their own advice.

As we saw in the last section, adults sometimes don't behave as fairly, kindly, or sensibly as they might like kids to think—and when it comes to something as serious as climate change, that's a big problem. Because while people are stuck in arguments that just go around and around in circles, the climate crisis keeps steaming ahead.

Think about how your actions affect others.

Listen when people are talking.

Remember to share!

We need to find ways to move forward together, positively and efficiently, with as many people as possible doing what they can to help. We're all human, which means that none of us are perfect, but by "doing as adults say, not as they do," young people might be able to make a lot more progress in fixing climate change—and teach adults how to do the same.

Climate change is such a huge issue that it can be hard to know where to begin. It might even make you feel so anxious, sad, or hopeless that you sometimes feel like it's not even worth trying to solve it at all. Over the next few pages, we'll look at some ways you can help make a big difference by following what seem to be pretty basic ideas.

The most important thing to remember is that no one person can solve climate change by themselves. You don't need to be the world's greatest expert, or a perfect eco-saint who always makes the "greenest" choices. That's just not realistic for most people, and we need "most people" on board.

Think about the changes you can make in your own everyday life and in the wider world. Discover your strengths and use them to work effectively with others. And when things feel tough, which they sometimes will, remember that we're all working for something truly amazing—a version of our planet that's better than anyone alive today has ever seen.

Do your best

Adults love telling kids "Just do your best," don't they? To be fair, it's good advice for tackling climate change, because although everyone in the world can do their bit, our efforts will look pretty different.

For example, the average person living in a rich country is responsible for a lot more emissions than the average person in a poorer country. That means that on average they can do more to reduce their impact—such as trying to shop, eat meat, drive, and use plastic less often.

Just like countries, not all people can contribute equally.

Doing your best is based on your personal effort, not how the results compare to anyone else.

Don't worry about finishing the job—it's about making a start.

Of course, not everyone lives like this imaginary "average person," and these changes are much harder for some people to make. That's OK—You don't need to solve all the problems at once or have an answer for everything. In the fight against climate change, every contribution is valuable.

"Doing your best" isn't just about trying to do it all on your own, either. When we work together with others, even in a pretty small group, we can create change on a much bigger scale. For example, what changes could you and your classmates get your school to make so it causes less harm to the environment?

Keep an eye out in your local area for opportunities to take action, too, from volunteering at a community garden to joining campaigns against nature-destroying new developments. You could look into joining national or international youth climate action movements. Think about what your strengths and skills are—anything from drawing to organizing events—and how you can use them to help.

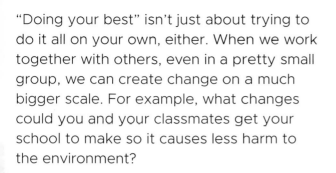

Whatever you can do, no matter how small, helps people already suffering from climate change.

Don't wait for others to lead—jump right in with your own strengths and skills!

Climate activism is a marathon, not a sprint—like an athlete, your "best" will change over time as you learn and do more. Give yourself time to build up to it, so you don't end up too exhausted and frustrated to continue—you could even keep a diary to track your progress over time.

Think BIG

It might be a bit overwhelming when adults tell you to focus on the "bigger picture" of your life, rather than minor disappointments or petty arguments. But they're right! And the same applies to climate change.

People who care about the environment can often feel really guilty when they do something they know isn't very "green," such as buying something in plastic packaging. But guess what, nobody's perfect all the time!

Your time and energy are precious—use them in the way that will make the biggest difference!

Politicians and businesses can make it easier for everyone to make good choices.

When responsibility for climate change is all pushed onto individuals, we can get stuck playing the "blame game," which distracts us from the responsibility that businesses and governments need to take. Their actions can have effects on a much larger scale than our choices as individuals, and they can also make eco-friendly choices much easier and more achievable for a wider range of people.

For instance, a great way to boost the number of cyclists is to spend money on cycling **infrastructure**. That means creating lots of safe, joined-up bike routes, so more people feel confident enough to give it a try. It makes much more sense to put pressure on the government to do this, rather than scolding drivers about not cycling when they might feel it's too difficult or dangerous to try.

Remember that heroes through history changed the world by taking bold steps and showing leadership.

If you have a powerful job or position in society, your actions have a big impact— set a good example!

Governments can also introduce laws to stop businesses from making and selling eco-unfriendly products, so shoppers don't have to work so hard to avoid them. But that doesn't mean businesses need to wait to be told what to do. Business people with good ideas have always tried to change the way we live—they can lead the way on the environment too.

It's only natural that we talk to our friends and family about climate change, and try to get them to change their habits. But think about this: you could tell ten people to drive less... or you could get those ten people to help you campaign for better public transportation and get EVERYONE to drive less.

Ask questions

Helpful adults will encourage you to ask lots of questions—it's one of the best ways to learn. To solve the climate crisis, we need to keep questioning everything and acting on what we discover.

The way the world works isn't set in stone, and it's important to question why things are the way they are—and how they can be better. Over the last 200 years, the people with the most power to shape the world have gotten things so wrong that we're on track to destroy Earth—and ourselves—unless we make serious changes.

To solve the climate crisis, we need to ask some big questions about the values that got us into this mess. Why is making money seen as more important than protecting our planet? If all humans are supposed to have equal rights, why do some people have so much more power than everyone else?

We also need to question what information we can trust. When expert climate scientists work out statistics and suggest solutions, it's based on evidence from carefully checked research, so we know it's as reliable as possible. But the media, particularly the internet, is also full of incorrect, misleading, and unproven claims and "facts" about climate change that go against what these experts say.

Sometimes this false information comes from people who don't properly understand climate science and want to deny its scary reality. But polluting industries—and investors profiting from them—also have the money and power to spread misinformation widely and get people on their side. Another issue is people getting overexcited about technology offering us easy solutions to climate change—we need to question how effective, safe, and realistic these "magic fixes" really are.

Everyone—including you—deserves an equal say on the future of our planet.

Be wary of easy answers. We need to make big changes to how our world works.

FILL YOUR WATER BOTTLE

Get in the habit of asking lots of questions and being suspicious of easy answers and claims that aren't backed up with proper evidence. Don't be put off by people who say "That's just the way things are," either—it's exactly what people who like things the way they are want you to think.

Try to understand

It can be incredibly frustrating when people don't seem to care about fixing climate change. What reasons could people possibly have for wanting things to stay the same while the planet burns around us? The answer is: lots of reasons.

Many people care about climate change just as much as you, but they're busy and exhausted from their day-to-day lives. They just don't have the time and energy to worry about an issue as huge as climate change, especially when they need to deal with more immediate problems such as how to pay the rent or bills.

To some people, worrying about something that isn't affecting you right this minute looks like a luxury.

Or the changes we have to make might threaten people's sense of identity, which may be tied up with interests such as cars, traveling abroad, and keeping up with fashion trends. How would you feel if someone ordered you to never listen to your favorite music again? Or give up your strongest beliefs? People never react well if you act like their interests are less important than yours.

Before you tell people what to do, imagine how it'd feel to give up the things you care about most.

People might be too scared to fully acknowledge the reality of climate change, especially if they've heard comforting false news reports telling them that it's exaggerated or not real at all, and that nothing really needs to change. Wouldn't it be nice to think that was true? It's not surprising many people prefer to think that way, even when faced with the science that tells them it isn't.

However strongly you feel about climate change, you need to listen to people who don't share your views. You don't have to agree with them, but if you don't try to understand where they're coming from, then why should they listen to you? People have emotional and practical reasons for not supporting climate action, and shouting scientific **evidence** at them isn't going to win them around. You might hear the science, but they just hear the shouting.

Making big changes can feel risky— it's only human to be scared.

If you want to convince someone, understanding where they're coming from is a good start.

Climate activists want people to face up to a really scary reality full of danger and big changes— and often to give up their own time, convenience, and comfort. That's a lot to ask! So along with the scientific evidence, we need to show people a lot of respect, patience, and understanding.

Make things fair

The world isn't fair, but that doesn't mean it should stay that way. Adults encourage kids to share and to treat each other fairly, but sadly they don't always apply this to their own lives.

Climate change doesn't affect everyone equally—in fact, the countries and people who have done the least to cause climate change often suffer the most from its effects. This makes existing inequalities even worse, pushing an even greater burden onto those who are already discriminated against, such as black and **indigenous** people, and people with disabilities. Unfair, right? That's why the idea of climate justice is so important.

Climate justice is all about recognizing this unfairness and trying to make things right. Rather than only concentrating on the "science side" of the climate crisis, we need to work toward creating a more equal world where everyone's human rights are respected. This means our climate "solutions" have to be both effective and fair—if they only tick the first box, that's not good enough, and they need more work.

WE CARE

Richer countries need to acknowledge that they've done more to create the climate crisis than others.

Climate solutions need to feel fair to everybody—not just the people in charge.

It's important to remember that fair doesn't always mean equal. Poorer countries often find it unfair that they're expected to take equal responsibility for the climate crisis when many rich countries got rich partly by using polluting industries to boost their economy. On a smaller scale, too, if climate action puts people in an unfairly difficult position, they will probably resent and reject it.

For instance, raising taxes on car fuel without guaranteeing widespread, affordable public transportation would unfairly affect poorer people in certain areas. Many people also worry about losing their jobs in polluting industries, so governments need to provide new jobs by supporting and investing in green businesses and infrastructure: eco-friendly houses, rail networks, renewable energy, and more.

In order for plans for climate action to be accepted and therefore successful, everyone involved must believe that they're fair. This means providing for countries and communities that are more seriously affected by climate change, asking different countries to take appropriate amounts of responsibility, and making sure that solutions include positive steps such as new jobs and transport systems.

Listen carefully

It sometimes feels like adults are contantly telling kids to 'Ssssshhh!' and 'Listen!' But listening carefully to what others have to say really is important, especially when it comes to climate action.

In the media, efforts to solve climate change are often shown as being led by a small number of well-off people in rich countries. But that's wrong! People all over the world, from all backgrounds, are leading important campaigns and sharing vital knowledge and viewpoints—it's just that many of them are being ignored.

We need to respect and listen to people from all countries and all backgrounds—not ignore or silence them.

In an unfair world set up to favor certain, **privileged** voices, "listening" has to be more active than you might think. Rather than just paying attention to the climate movement's most famous figures and groups, dig deeper! For example, you could ask a parent or guardian to help you search online—particularly on social media—to find youth activists from marginalized communities and poorer countries.

Remember that there is no "one size fits all" way to take climate action.

So what actions could help more people hear a diverse range of voices? A good place to start is sharing climate activists' names, ideas, and achievements so others can benefit from them, too. You could keep track of your learning in a notebook or a folder on a computer and present what you've found out—maybe at school, or in a meeting of a local action group.

Rich countries have to take some responsibility for pollution that other countries create on their behalf.

You can also ask an adult to help you find out about campaigns aimed at stopping deliberate attempts to bully, scare, and silence people—both online and offline. Some brave activists and journalists take huge risks to fight climate change, facing threats or even attacks. The more attention we can bring to their struggles, the harder it is for people to get away with trying to stop them.

Climate change isn't a future problem; it's already seriously affecting many people—often the poorest and most vulnerable.

When people are silenced or ignored, everyone loses the opportunity to gain the knowledge they have to share. By listening carefully, you'll probably come across points that you'd never thought about before—and rethink some others you already believed.

Use your imagination

Sometimes we all get bored or stuck for ideas and fall back on doing the same things we've always done. But using your imagination can give you a boost to keep on fighting climate change.

Many people are so used to living in a world that puts profits before people and the planet, they can't really imagine things being any different. Unimaginative thinking suits the people making fortunes from our current systems—they want things to stay just as they are.

Solving the climate crisis makes economic sense in the long run—there's no "business as usual" on a destroyed planet.

That's where your imagination comes in. See something you don't like, such as world hunger, or polluted oceans? Imagining a future without it is the first step to figuring out how we get there.

Being able to imagine a different world, to hold it in your mind and believe that it could exist someday soon—that's a powerful thing. Of course, some people will get annoyed when you do this and call you "unrealistic." But 200 years ago, those people would have told you it was unrealistic to imagine slavery being abolished, women having the right to vote, or same-sex couples getting married...

So never be embarassed about dreaming of a better world. It's the people who think things can continue as they are who are being unrealistic!

Let's use the knowledge and resources we already have more imaginatively, rather than relying on untested technologies.

Don't be discouraged by what others do— imagine a better world and take action to make it a reality.

Let's use our imaginations to rethink what "wealth" actually means. The Earth is all we have, and it gives us air to breathe, water to drink, food to eat, and other resources for everything from clothes to medicine. That makes it more precious than any amount of money, right? We need to build a new world that reflects this reality.

Keep it simple

If you ever feel overwhelmed by the whirlwind of school, friends, news, fashion, trends, social media, and more, someone may have told you to "Relax," "Keep it simple," and "Remember what's really important." The same applies to the climate crisis.

Humans need a few essential things to survive—food, water, air, shelter, and enough clothes to stay warm. We also all need and deserve things that make us truly happy and fulfilled, like love, safety, freedom, education, rest, and healthcare. What none of us need—however much ads and celebrity **endorsements** try to convince us we do—is to constantly shop for newer, bigger, pricier, and more fashionable stuff.

Rethink what success looks like—it should be about the good you're doing, not the money and 'stuff' that you have.

Everyone needs to shop and travel sometimes, just think about how to make it as eco-friendly as possible.

But today, most countries' economies are based on producing and selling more, more, more—and so companies encourage people to buy more, more, more. Earth simply can't keep up with the scale and speed of all this, and to solve the climate crisis we need to rein it all in.

If it feels like everyone around you is buying new, cool stuff all the time, it's easy to get swept up in envy and anxiety and think you'll miss out by not doing the same. But try not to get distracted by all these exciting, shiny promises of happiness. By keeping things simple and focusing your time and energy on helping to save the Earth and all the people and animals that depend on it, you'll find a much deeper, long-lasting satisfaction.

Try not to get distracted, either, by the idea that technology will step in to save us all from the climate crisis. It's great that people are trying to find clever solutions to fight climate change, but we can't rely on untested technologies. They could end up not working, causing unexpected and serious problems, or being too expensive to help on a large scale—especially in poorer countries that are hardest hit by climate change.

Focus on what you can do, rather than worrying about how that compares to everyone else—you might inspire them!

Don't wait for new technologies to solve the climate crisis. Do what you can to make a difference now.

Solving the climate crisis means taking a hard look at what's really important. If we want a safe and healthy planet for ourselves and future generations, one that can provide us with real essentials like food, water, and clean air, we have to step away from shopping and hi-tech dreaming and instead work together to make big changes.

Work together

Everyone has a part to play in stopping climate change. By working together we can be sure our efforts will make a difference.

Whichever part you play—wherever you find yourself in this picture (and that might be on several different levels)—you'll be part of the solution. You can spread the word about climate science, justice, and action. You can praise politicians and companies taking genuinely positive steps and protest against those that don't. You can tell adults exactly what they can do to support you, and inspire them to keep going when they're feeling worn out from the struggle against climate change.

If people across the world come together to stand up for ourselves and our planet, we can stop climate change and build a fairer world at the same time. Adults are in charge now, but the future is yours—and you can be so much more powerful than you might think.

What will you do? And how will you influence others to do their best, too?

We will find solutions to scientific problems

We will shout until something gets done

We will make good choices every day

GLOSSARY

absorb Take in or soak up, like a sponge soaks up water

acidic More likely to react with other substances in a way that can harm life

activist Someone who spends time fighting for a cause they believe in

animal products Things we get from animals, such as meat, milk, or wool

carbon dioxide Gas produced by burning (and animals breathing) that contributes to the greenhouse effect

carbon leakage An increase in emissions in one country because of a decrease in another

carbon offsetting Doing something such as planting trees that hopefully cancels out the emissions you're responsible for

carbon sink Something that takes lots of carbon dioxide out of the atmosphere, such as a forest

climate resilience The ability to survive climate change with minimal harm

consumers Members of the public who buy things

consumption Buying and using things

crude oil Liquid pumped from the ground that is made into gasoline and other fuels

data Collection of facts or measurements used to tell us something about the world

democracy A form of government where people regularly get to choose their leaders

drought Long period of dry weather when crops die and food runs low

economy The sum of all the buying, selling, and making in a country, and a measure of its wealth

ecosystems Collections of living things that interact in the same place

efficiently Using as little energy or effort as possible

emissions Release of harmful gases

endorsements Paid recommendations from famous people to sell a product

evidence Objects or facts that prove something is true (or untrue)

fossil fuel Substance such as coal that was created millions of years ago and is dug out of the ground and burned for energy

geoengineering Technology designed to alter the Earth's weather or other natural processes

import Buy or bring in goods or services from another country

indigenous People such as Native Americans who lived in a land before the arrival of settlers

infrastructure Networks for transporting people, or things they need, such as electricity and water

insulated Wrapped in a heat-proof layer, to keep warm or cool

investors People who lend money to companies in return for a future share of the money they make

landfill Getting rid of rubbish by burying it in the ground

lobbyists People paid by an organization to put pressure on governments into taking particular actions

media Ways of communicating that reach lots of people, such as TV or websites

migrants People who have left their home country or region to live elsewhere

ozone layer A gas layer that protects the Earth from harmful rays from the Sun

packaging Disposable wrapping or container that protects and preserves a product until it's used

predict Try to say what will happen in the future, based on your knowledge

privileged Having more wealth or power than other people

process Turn a raw material into a finished product

profits The extra money left over when businesses have paid for staff, materials, and other costs

public transportation Shared, government-run ways of getting around, such as buses or trains

recycle Turn back into a raw material to use again

renewable Lasting forever without running out

satellites Spacecrafts that loop around the Earth in a fixed pattern

spokesperson Someone paid by an organization to explain its views in public

subsidies Money given by governments to help certain industries or to keep prices low

SUV Sport utility vehicle—a large, heavy car that uses lots of energy

taxes Money charged by the government to pay for things and change behavior

unilateral Acting alone without waiting for others to agree

unsustainable Not able to last forever

INDEX